HEALTHY RELATIONSHIPS

The Fundamental Pocket Guide

Rose W. Muraguri (BEd., MA)

© 2013

Healthy Relationships: The Fundamental Pocket Guide

Copyright ©2013: Rose W. Muraguri

Candor Books

1001 Navaho Dr. Suite 109.
Raleigh, NC, 27609. USA.

ISBN: 13: 978-1461038788

Printed in the United States of America

Acknowledgements

I would like to thank the conveners of "Smart Marriages" whose conferences I attended from 2007 to 2010 and where I saw practical relationship skills at work. I particularly thank *The Dibble Institute* and *IDEALS-NIRE* whose workshops inspired me.

I am also indebted to the many young people who agreed to apply of the simple principles in this guide in their relationships and for sharing their experiences with me. I felt honored for allowing me to influence their lives in building blocks for healthy relationships. Out of their shared experiences, I feel confident that this practical guide is essential to our readers exploring their own love relationships.

This guide would not have seen the light of day were it not for my dear husband Robert, who was passionate about my work and encouraged me all through. I am also very grateful to our daughters Christine, Quincy and Pressy who have incessantly given me invariable insights to the world of teenagers and young adults of the present era.
I thank the Almighty God, for without his power I can achieve nothing.

Rose Muraguri

Table of Contents

Preface

Love is a central feature in almost every person's life. Some people have said that love is blind while others describe love as breaking all barriers may they be of color, race, creed or faith, class or status. This is possibly because man was created as a loving being, and out of love. Therefore love is a beautiful thing and is to be cherished by all who experience it. Love is wrapped up in relationships and so to enjoy that love, one will have take care of the wholesome friendship.

I have worked closely with both young and older people in relationships. There is a conflict between how these two groups view relationships. This is particularly true between parents and their teens or young adults. Young people often feel greatly misunderstood and judged in how they engage and handle relationships. So when they have questions about relationships or are experiencing a difficult time, many do not say a word to their parents or counselors. This book is designed to help them make and maintain healthy love relationships.

Friendship and relationships are more likely to thrive when the people involved take control. So this pocket guide is for you in relationship and those who will be getting into love relations in the future. It empowers you to take control of your relationship. It explores some simple facts about creating a healthy relationship. It is about making your relationship fun without burdening yourself with too many obligations too early.

This guide uses some probe questions that any person considering a relationship should ask themselves to have the best chance of a fun, enjoyable and successful relationship. So if you have questions and you feel like you do not have somebody to confide in, your options to a successful relationship are in here, and you need not panic.

The book is divided into 3 parts. Part 1 is about the facts of love and relationships. Part 2 is about self evaluation with tools which can be very helpful when applied with honesty. It also points out what an abusive relationship looks like and what one can do about it. Often love relations will involve partying and driving. Part 3 explores challenges of driving, partying and how to think outside the box. Some items discussed in Part 3 are more applicable to drivers in the Western world; however anybody who sits behind the wheel has friends and or owns a mobile phone should pay attention.

This book can also be used by older people whose relationships continue to radiate the energy and romance of youth and by those who may be experiencing some turbulence in their love life.

Rose W. Muraguri, BEd., MA (Marriage & Family), 2013

Part 1: Love & Relationships

Let's talk about love and relationships.

If you ask many young people how they are fairing in relationships today, many will simply tell you that they are fine. Some find it hard to discuss what they may be going through especially with an older person whom they feel is a little too old to understand. Others will say they are fine because they are having fun sometimes, yet others will say the relationship is great even when they are having problems because that is the cool thing to say.

Do you remember those years that you sat and waited by the phone hoping he will call, or even made up this imaginary girlfriend or boyfriend that you told all your friends about. This is because everybody wants to be loved and accepted. So before you draw a pointing finger and say the young generation has gone haywire on relationships, let us explore some facts with them.

Healthy relationships require some thinking, evaluation, tact and skill. Before you push this guide away, and say you've heard it all before, think about this. Ever seen a football or basketball player (or any other sport) who is so successful? Did they just hit the field and became a success overnight? No, they put a lot of thought, purpose, discipline and practice into it. They had to learn the skills to help them.

Likewise, there are skills that are learned to help people choose the kind of relationships that are likely to be successful. It would be foolish to just expect a relationship to be great because you happened to be in it. Even if it starts as love at first sight, you have to nurture it and be thoughtful if it is going to succeed. We will be looking at some very basic things you can use to evaluate your situation and see if you are in a healthy relationship. At times, you may need to exit (or end) a relationship.

Think about it this way, everyone can fit in one of these categories about relationships.

- One is either in a relationship and not sure about the future of the relationship, (possibly trying to end it but do not know how).
- Not in a relationship at all
- In a relationship they feel quite committed to with promise of a future together.

What is your relationship category?

_____

_____

Like other life skills, relationships require a vision.

Vision: Do I have one?

Everyone needs to have a vision

A vision is a mind picture of what one desires: you envision your life

Focusing on a vision helps guide your choices and actions

Having a vision motivates you to move forward: from where you are to where you want to be.

Examples of visions

John: Finish College and get a great job

Jane: Be the head pastor of a great church

Mary: Start a business and employ dozens of people

Pearl: Visit the space, and be a pilot

Meg: Start a line of designer shoes

Jack: Marry and have a great family

Me:

_____

_____

The vision you have for your life will influence the decisions you make

Choices: Your Life is not Neutral

You have to make decisions about many aspects of your life; ignoring, postponing or refusing to decide does not take away your responsibility to decide, you will have to do it sooner or later.

Life is not Neutral!

Decisions made in relationships have implications in other aspects of life

Decisions you make in relationships are important: they will affect all other aspects of your life either directly or indirectly.

13

Increase your chances of being in a smart relationship

Learn about yourself: all effective relations start with you.

How do I see myself?

List down words that describe you. Be honest with yourself.

Example: Fun to be with, honest, hard working.

_____

_____

What are my expectations? (How do I want things to be, and how do I think things should be?)

Acknowledge that you have expectations and it is a good thing, otherwise life would just be happening to you.

Here are some hints to help you think and write out your expectations: School -what level of education do I want to achieve? -High school diploma? Associate degree? Bachelor's, Master's degree, a different kind of training?

Career, work, romance, family, friends, money, pregnancy, communication, faith, health, diseases, etc

Now write down what your expectations are, you may write a few and add others later.

Education: _____

Faith/Religion: _____

Work/Career: _____

Be realistic-What do I do with these expectations?

Examine your expectations and decide what is realistic.

Discuss them with a close friend or family member to see if the expectations are reasonable

Communicate your expectations to the person(s) concerned.

You have to be willing to work to meet your expectations.

Do I need to make changes to stay on vision?

Now think: Who do I hang out with, is that the right company? Do I spend too much time on computer, phone, TV? Are some of these behaviors slowing or preventing me from pursuing my vision?

Write down the things that take up most of your free time.

_____

_____

Write down things that you know you need to change in order for you to stay on vision and meet your expectations.

_____

_____

Gain some knowledge about your friend or partner
Choose greens versus reds.

Many teenagers go into relationships *"blindfolded"*. If you were blindfolded and then given two bowls, one with red candy and the other with green, and red represented poor relationship while green represents healthy relationship, how would you make sure you choose from the green bowl?

_____

_____

What if bowl one had about 85% green and 15% red, and bowl 2 had the opposite, 15% green and 85% red? How can you increase your likelihood of choosing a green candy?

_____

_____

(Write down your answers, and then compare with answers at the back).

Now that you have compared your answers, you may be wondering how you get to *remove the blindfold.* What we are going to discuss next is how you get to know whether you are in the right relationship or not. Even if you fell in love at first sight, you can use these check points to help you know if you need to stay or exit the relationship. You would rather yank yourself out, even if you don't want to, than regret later.

What are you looking for in a relationship?

STOP and check this out: You cannot be logical if you are trying to evaluate your relationship while holding hands with your friend, taking a walk or you are in the same room enjoying a movie. The point is that the *chemistry* in your brain will stop you from being logical. So you need to be in a safe place, away from him/her, when your mind is calm, and reflect on the relationship.

 ALL successful relationships address or revolve around the following principles.

Common interests- a good match will have some common interests as you: List at least 5 of your top interests and his/hers and compare them.

Yours:

_____

_____

His/hers:

_____

_____

Common:

_____

_____

Values-the core values like religious beliefs must not be in conflict with yours? How does he/she see things like drugs, sex, and alcohol?

Yours:

_____

_____

His/hers:

_____

Common:

_____

_____

Communication: Is s/he a person you enjoy talking to?

_____

Is it easy to talk your thoughts with him/her, or are your conversations difficult and cautious?

_____

Expect healthy communication and willingness to improve from your partner. Do you see your partner as one willing to work to improve communication? Yes/No

Why?

_____

Even when you disagree, do you maintain respect for each other?

_____

Respect- Set standards of what you expect and stick by them. List the four most important things you consider respectful and you expect your partner to observe in your relationship.

_____

List four things you consider disrespectful and you cannot tolerate in a relationship.

_____

Don't change yourself just to win or keep friendship unless they are real changes you need to make. List things about you that you would like your friend to notice and admire

_____

Do not try to change the other person into someone they are not. Is he/she what you admire in personality and character or a fantasy of what you would like?

List what attracts you?

_____

_____

Do not put pressure on your friend and do not agree to be
pressured. Do you feel like your friend does things to
make you feel jealous, insecure or uncomfortable? Do you
feel used? List down 3 things you consider being
pressured.

_____

_____

_____

Three sides of a relationship

Chemistry

Love is chemically mediated; many teen and youth relationships start with chemistry.

Love chemicals in the brain sends you to a euphoria; your mind is reeling and you may not see (or hear) clearly. A friend, parent or relative asking you to watch yourself seems like the greatest enemy, or at least jealous. This could be beginning of love, or maybe not. Do NOT read too much in your love feelings. It is the easiest time to fall into a risky or poor relationship. Some young people slide into sex or physical intimacy which they often regret later.

Chemistry is an important part of relationship, it is passionate; you feel attractive, wonderful, indescribable. That is ok, enjoy the feeling BUT take it slow, shake yourself back to reality.

Stay in open areas, or in company of friends and relatives

If you are spending time alone with him or her take a walk in the park, or downtown, go to city stadium, go see a movie or other open places. You can enjoy time just the two of you, yet you are surrounded by people.

Avoid secluded places, his or your bedroom, home just the two of you; avoid a drive to dark or unlit places. Write what you would find safe and unsafe while friendship is in its early stages.

Brain action is chemical

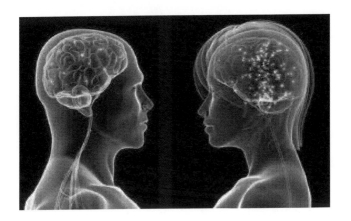

Levels of intimacy: Make boundaries

Permitted/Safe	Banned/Unsafe
Light hugs	Touching under clothes
Holding hands	Passionate kiss
Gentle / hand kiss	Sex / physical intimacy

Friendship

This is an important part of a relationship too. This is when you get to know your friend a little more, the things that you share:

- Are you able to talk to each other freely?
- Do you enjoy being in the company of each other, doing fun things that are not physical?
- Does he/she care about your school/ homework or your interests?
- Does he/she respect your friends, parents, relatives?
- Does he/she value your opinions on issues?
- Do you spend enough time apart? Does s/he let you spend time with your other friends, relatives, family? This is an important boundary and balance to keep.
- Is s/he ever on the phone with you when you are not together? This can be both exhausting and controlling. Each of you needs time apart.

A friend will care about you as a wholesome person, without seeking to control. S/he will encourage and support you in pursuing your life goals. If they tell you that school, work, your relatives, your old friends, your family do not matter; think twice, it is a red flag in your relationship.

List activities that you enjoy/would enjoy doing with your very close friend.

_____

_____

Commitment and trust

This is the third side of a relationship and it is equally important

Many teenagers and young people relationships may not get to experience the fullness of this stage, and that is ok because they are not ready to commit. They have many other live goals to achieve and will be happy to remain as good friends, or boyfriend/ girlfriend.

Commitment comes as relationship becomes deeper and two people feel they trust each other. Commitment involves an intention to share a future, to provide each other with mutual support and be faithful. They are possibly for people who may be planning of marriage. Trust and commitment comes with the maturity of a relationship and this takes time and nurturing, it should not be hurried. Many people do not reach this level until they are in their twenties

It is possible and very healthy to experience romantic relationship without engaging in sex. Sex before marriage complicates issues. Many cultures of the world, including in Africa, Europe and America, put the context of healthy sexual relations in marriage.

Relationship pyramid

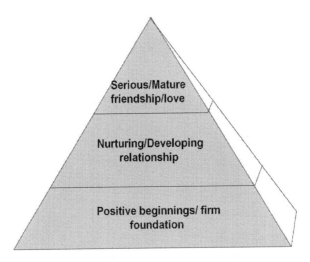

Write things you can do or say to build each of the three stages of healthy relationship

Firm Foundation	Strengthening Relationship	Indicators of Maturity

Inverted pyramid

Remember that if you are not in a relationship yet, it is a good time to lay the ground rules you will need to observe when you get into one. If you are in relationship too, you can do the same. If there are things that happened that you already regret, do not dwell on that too much, reexamine your relationship and move on. This may mean continuing with the relationship but applying your new standards or exiting the relationship.

In short, no matter what other boundaries you set, it is paramount not to engage in sexual or physical intimacy before relationship gets to the mature stage which in many cases it is marriage.

What if the relationship that sweeps you off the ground is not going to last, as often happens? You do not want to have engaged in sex which you will later regret. If you have this in mind way before any relationship begins, then you are most likely to stay safe. If you are trying to think about boundaries at the spur of the moment, the chemistry in your mind and body is likely to give way and you will very likely not be able to be assertive in staying away from sex.

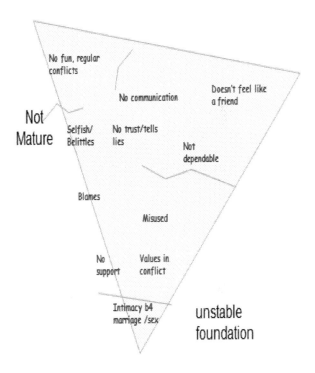

List activities that are fun and safe	List activities that are a no go zone

Exercise: This is important and you can take a couple of days to think about it. It will help you to be objective when you evaluate or reflect on your relationship.

Think about a relationship of a couple that you have seen that seem to be doing well in the three different sides of a relationship.

Chemistry: You admire the romantic side of their relationship: List the specific things you see that make their chemistry strong _____

Friendship: _____

Commitment: _____

Part 2: Relationships Checklist

Stepping in with the basics

Now that you know what a healthy relationship should look like and what to look for, it is time to think about your relationship if you are in one or how you would like your future relationship to be like.

You can also think about a close friendship you have, not necessarily a girl/boyfriend relationship because the same basics apply.

Why you should be careful

A wrong relationship will make you feel more alone than when you were single.

Is it Infatuation? OR Is it true friendship/Love?

Infatuation	Love/true friendship?
Focused on looks and attraction- (Is he/her too focused on your dressing, make up, looks, and even sometimes make you feel uncomfortable?)	**Focuses on the whole person** (Though interested in your looks and attracted, s/he is also interested in your school, work, friends, your likes, fun activities, etc)
More of acting to conform. (Do you fear that if s/he really knows you the way you really are you might lose him/her? Do you act and pretend to be what s/he likes you to be? Do	**Is confidence building** (You act and behave like yourself; you do not do things just to please somebody to stay in a relationship. You also feel s/he likes you just the way you are and you feel sure

you worry s/he might find out more about you and dump you?)	of yourself.)
Is controlling Does s/he keep calling and checking on what you are doing almost all the time? What about trying to keep you away from your other friends and relatives? Kind of isolate you?	**Gives personal space** Respects your personal space and time, so you spend time together and you spend time apart. Respects that you still have family, friends, and your own schedules to follow.
It is a rushed affair Infatuation makes things to happen at a very fast pace. It is like all is happening at once and	**Love is gradual** You get to know the person gradually, by talking and doing fun activities together. As you

you do not have time for other things or people. Your emotions are strong even before you get to know him /her well.	learn more about him/her you get to connect more and may be fall in love.
Infatuation is jealous Is s/he jealous that you have other friends? Or are you worried that's/he may drop you because of his/her friends and so wants him/her to cut off those friendships? Do you feel insecure in the relationship?	**Love involves trust, it brings security** In love or true friendship you enjoy each other's friends without being suspicious or jealous. It makes you feel happy, comfortable and secure even around his/her friends.
Feels like a lot of work sometimes	**Enjoy each other's company and friendship**

Infatuation sometimes make you feel weary, it is like you have to do so much to keep the relationship.	Love looks forward to spending time together; it is like you do not have to prepare so much to be with your friend.
Can lead you to do things you know are wrong (Does s/he ask you to try out alcohol/drugs/to lie to your parents so that you can be with him, to skip classes? etc) Does s/he try to talk you into thinking or doing something that you know deep down in your heart that it is wrong?	**You are more likely to do the things you believe to be right** Love encourages you to do what is right for you and others, and you friend will encourage and respect this.

Dating

Dating is a fine thing to do and relationships cannot grow without dating. One however needs to do it at a comfortable age and with some knowledge on how to go about it. In many instances, casual friendships may develop into serious relationships and there may be no clear cut line on when dating starts. This is fine because it means the individuals have grown into the relationship. They may however need to use some helpful tips if for example they are in school and do not want to take their relationship to the next level yet.

Be aware: Know if you are dating

Many teenagers start dating without realizing that they are dating. Some refuse to recognize it as dating and call it other names especially if they do not want parents or family members to know.

Research results of dating relationships show that 72% of 8th & 9th graders date I

Dating violence

Dating Violence is a phenomenon experienced all across the board, meaning it affects people of all races, classes, income, education and color. So do not associate it to others, it could happen to anyone. You therefore need to be informed on how to identify the danger signs that can lead to DV and learn what to do to avoid the situation and help others.

Teens and young adults are at a greater risk mostly because they are relatively new in relations and also because there are many changes happening to their bodies and therefore are blinded to some facts of life.

Girls and women are also said to be at a greater risk of injury while men and boys are often the perpetrators. That being said, it does not mean that boys and men are not abused and therefore they too need to be aware and know how to protect themselves.

Teen Dating Violence is common- very important to make sure you know when a relationship is turning unhealthy

It is a pattern of unhealthy behaviors in a teen dating (going out with a friend) also called:

- Dating violence
- Intimate partner violence especially when it involves young people or adults in relationships
- For married people it comes in form of domestic violence

Danger signs in a relationship

Physical violence

- Pinching and kicking
- Slapping or hitting
- Shoving or shaking
- Grabbing or throwing

Emotional violence

- Humiliating or embarrassing

- Controlling and belittling

- Withholding Information

- Isolating: Be very aware, this happens to many people

- Stalking or tracking your whereabouts all the time.

Sexual violence

- Unwanted touching: It is not ok, it is not love

- Pressuring or forced sexual acts

- Threats if you refuse to abide to their sexual demands

- Taking inappropriate photos of you or themselves

Electronic violence

- Electronic messages and images can be destructive, beware of inappropriate photos sent to you.

- Text, posts, internet activity that can impact on relationship, be careful what you post

- Use of cyber systems to bully, embarrass, abuse or do any other unpleasant things

Did you know?

- 1 in every 4 adolescents report verbal, physical, or emotional abuse by a boy/girl friend

- On college campuses, intimate partner violence is one of the most frequent causes of injury

- 85% of reported cases of dating violence are committed by men against women

- One out of every three women murdered is killed by a current or ex boyfriend or husband.

- Women ages 16-24 experience the highest rates of intimate violence

- 68% of young women who experience rape know their rapist as a boyfriend, friend, or casual acquaintance.

- 40% of teens, ages 14 to 17 say they know someone about their age who has been hit or beaten by their boyfriend.

- About 60% of victims of abuse do not seek help.

Physical signs of Injury

If you see a friend having any, some or all of the following signs, Urgent help is needed:

- Truancy, dropping out of school

- Sudden drop in grades

- Changes in mood and or personality for the worse

43

- Unwanted pregnancy

- Complains on health issues/ headaches

- Emotional outburst

- Wanting to keep alone/isolation

- General body malaise/ Stress

- Suicidal talk/thoughts

- Engagement in risky behavior

Relationship evaluation questions:

Just read the following questions and answer ***true*** or ***false*** as it relates to your friend in your relationship

- S/he texts me and calls so many times, whether night or day
- Says that I am involved in too many activities and would rather be together almost always
- Is jealous and does not like me talking to my other friends

- Accuses me and gets really angry when I hang out with my long time friends
- Is critical of my dressing and wants to influence or control what I wear
- Tries to isolate me from family and wants us to keep our relationship secret
- Does not like most of the things I do and criticize my choices
- Often blames me if things go wrong
- Is very secretive about his family and friends
- Makes me feel that I am worthless and no one would want me if s/he dropped me
- Often embarrasses or humiliates me in front of people but later apologizes
- Sometimes s/he pushes me, hits me/ shoves me
- When angry s/he can be so mean to me, even accusing me of things he knows are not true
- When angry s/he shouts at me but later apologizes and is really good to me

- He makes me feel like I am wrong most of the time
- Sometimes s/he ignores me and pretends he doesn't know me when s/he is with friends
- Does not thank me when I do something good
- Discourages me from trying new things and often says my dreams are ridiculous
- Makes me feel bad about some things I do for her/him even when s/he knows I tried my best
- Sometimes makes fun of presents I give him and makes me feel stupid
- Sometimes goes through my personal items or my phone
- Has trouble listening to me or holding a conversation
- Gets upset when I go visiting with family and friends and accuses me of neglecting him/her
- Intimidates me to choose between her/him and family

- Belittles my opinions and makes fun of my suggestions
- Very difficult for me to predict what his/her mood will be; s/he seems to change all the time
- When we disagree, s/he attacks my character instead of the issue at hand
- I feel unsafe when we argue and I am alone with him/her
- Often views my words and actions more negatively than I mean them to be
- Often makes plans of what s/he wants us to do without involving me and when I refuse, s/he says I am ungrateful
- S/he pressures me to take the relationship to a deeper level even when I say that I am not ready
- S/he insists we become physically/sexually intimate even though I have told him/her that is against my values to do this before marriage

- Sometimes I get scared of him/her even though I do not let him/her know
- I want to break up with her /him but I am afraid.

Remember that relationships can be healthy, unhealthy or somewhere in between. However, everybody is capable of engaging and building healthy relationships. It does not mean that if you answered *true* to very many questions that you are doomed. The extent or level to which every statement applies to your relationship will determine if you are in a potentially abusive relationship.

If you answered **True** to five or more questions and feel that these answers would score a 7/10 or above in intensity, I would suggest you seek help from someone you trust. Better be safe than sorry. You can ask to see a counselor who will discuss further your situation and help you see if you are in an abusive relationship or in danger of getting abused. He or she will help you see the level of your specific situation and will also discuss with you ways in which you can improve or save the relationship if that

48

is what you want. If it is more serious than you thought and you want to leave, the trusted adult or counselor will help you by giving you the options you have to do so safely.

A trusted adult, a counselor or a pastor will keep your information confidential and so you should have nothing to fear.

If you do not have a person to call or tell, call the National Domestic violence hotline at 1800-799-7233 or 1-866-331 9474 for peer advocates and assistance.

Why do people stay in abusive relationships?

Love: If you know somebody who is in an abusive relationship and they are not getting out, do not judge them but assist. It is very difficult to get out of relationships at times because even the abuser sometimes can be very nice and loving to their partner. The victim thinks and hopes that the abuse is over, because s/he wants the abuse to stop but not the relationship to be over.

Fear: some people fear that they may get harmed by their partners if they leave a relationship

Humiliation or embarrassment: some people may not want their friends or family to know about their situation and may opt to stay in an abusive situation than get out and feel embarrassed.

Other people have lived in around abusive situations and may think abusive is normal.

Lack of self confident and low self esteem: some people have stayed in the abusive situation where they are belittled and they think it is their fought that the relationship is not working.

Money: a victim may be relying on an abuser for financial assistance or other basic necessities.

Religious or cultural beliefs: Some beliefs will make some people to stay instead of risking shame for themselves and the family

Immigration Status: People who are undocumented fear that reporting abuse may affect their immigration status and they may fear being deported. Many abusers use this to threaten and mistreat their victims. If this is the case, victims should call the National domestic violence hotline, they will work with you to ensure you are safe without affecting your status.

Pregnancy or children: Sometimes people stay in abusive relations because they are pregnant and do not know what to do, or they have children and it becomes complicated to end the relationship.

In ALL these situations, there is help and there are options for the victims, that is why you need to read this and help others.

How can you help now that you have more information?

You can help a friend or family member whom you know is in an abusive relationship by:

Listening to them and offering them the options that they have, if you do not know how to do this, start them off by getting a helpline number, a counselor, a trusted adult or any options we discussed before.

Be available for them when they need to talk and listen with a non judgmental attitude

Listen and learn from people who have been victims of abuse. Stop abuse by advocating against it.

If somebody abuses his/her friend in your presence, do not act like they are doing a cool thing, disapprove of their action by saying you think that was a mean thing to say or do. If it is not safe to do so immediately, look for appropriate time to revisit the issue.

Part 3: Safety Matters

How does safety come in?

As mentioned in Part 1 of this pocket manual, love and relationships are chemically mediated. One common feature of this state is excitement and many schools of thought indicate that excited persons are prone to be irrational at times. It is therefore very important to consider your safety at every stage of the relationship. Is your partner leading you to unsafe situations? Is he or her concerned about your safety at every moment and situation that you are together, alone or with friends? This part gives you some basic safety checklists to guide you.

Driving check list:

Texting: In many States, it is now illegal to text while driving, (check the law in your State). Even where it is not, it is common sense that your safety and that of others on the road is of paramount importance. So you should simply stop any texting while driving, period.

Simply stop, you may already know texting that caused a life: if you do not, you do not want to be the example that will be quoted.

Alcohol use: Have you heard of crashes caused by teens or young people who were high on alcohol or other drugs? This is one of the surest ways to drive yourself and others to death, simply stop.

Call Somebody: If a friend is drunk, carefully and skillfully hide the keys from her or him, you can even help them "look" for the keys, as long as it takes long enough to have somebody sober come and drive you all home. Of course you will have used the "bathroom" from where you place that call to somebody to quickly come to your rescue.

What if you have nobody to call? Mary had nobody to call and her friends were drunk. She had even sneaked out to attend the party without her parent's permission. But when she saw that Mark was wobbling and planning to drive home, she called her parents, gave the address and soon they were rescued. Mary's father drove Mark and each of the teenager's to their homes. It was not party time for any of the parents or even the teenagers, but each one of them were very glad, that everybody was safe. You would rather get grounded than be on a hospital bed or worse still six feet under.

Ever considered calling the cops on yourself? This may sound crazy, but officers will help get you to your home safely, without a ticket. They care more about your safety, and they really would rather not fill up the jails if they can resolve the problem.

Too loud music: Jesse was driving with a team of his friends after celebrating a homecoming game. They were overjoyed and everybody was literally shouting over the blaring music. They had just dropped Rachel off were about to get onto the last exit when this huge van with its hazard lights started hooting nonstop and was moving at a very high speed, several cars were able to quickly get off its way. However none of the young people in Jesse's car saw or heard it, it was too late even as the van driver tried to maneuver his vehicle, his breaks had failed and it went crashing on Jesse's car. It was a sorry state, all four were severely injured. Justin commented on this hospital bed, "That damn music, wish it was not so loud, at least one of us could have heard the hooting!"

It does not matter who is on the wrong, but loud music has been known to cause distraction, reduce driver's attention on the road, or just reduce response time.

Company in car

Check the people you have in your car, or the ones you ride with. Some people are more disruptive than loud music. Friends who tease do or say things that make you want to turn and see instead of focusing your eyes on the road spell serious trouble. They can easily disrupt your concentration. Accidents happen within a split of a second, so be logical, neither you nor your friends are fun if they are dead.

So what do you do? Plan to meet at "that place", because they are fun to be with, but don't drive together. Possibly you would be behaving the same if they were driving, so they are good friends but the road is a not a respecter of age, occasion or situation, so be safe.

Sleep

It is one "drug" that many young and old ignore in relation to driving. While cops may test your level of alcohol in the body if they catch you in good time to prevent a possible accident, they cannot test your sleepiness. Yet many people have caused accidents because they dozed off just in a split of a second. Others are too tired that the mind is clogged with sleep and so their reaction time is slowed down. Whatever the case, do not drive while sleepy.

What can you do?

Pull up in a safe place like a gas station, stretch and get fresh air. If you are with a companion in the car who cannot drive and stretching does not help you, pull up and nap as needed while s/he keeps an eye.

You may go to a fast food place and take a break.

Who pays when we ignore these simple safety measures?

If an accident occurs:

All vehicle occupants: Injuries often occur and they have to deal with this

The driver: more often than not will be ticketed, earn points on his/her driving record or face charges

Families of injured: They may have to pay for hospital bills, call off work to offer care; others have to deal with death.

The State and or Federal Government: they have to dispatch police, paramedics, ambulances and sometimes mobilize the fire department.

Tax payers: We all pay taxes to keep government and State institutions running

Insurance companies: This will apply to both the injured and the damaged property

Friends and communities: Have you heard of a city, community, or school mourning the loss of a young teenager through a road accident that could have been avoided? The cases are too many. Both young and old need to be sensitive and proactive to stop them, I mean it is me and you that are going to make a difference.

The list could go on and on, but the key point is that accidents are both **expensive and strenuous**. They strain people physically, emotionally, financially and even spiritually. One accident may affect not just the individuals involved, but the family, possibly a whole school, the neighborhood.

Partying? Check list

- Are there actions or behavior you are uncomfortable with happening around you?
- Are you feeling pressured to do things you do not believe in?
- Is there alcohol or /and drug use even if you are not involved?
- Are there dirty jokes that make you feel a little uneasy?
- Are you and friends dressed in a way you would feel embarrassed if your parents or pastor saw you?
- Are you fearful or worried inside even though you are putting a strong face?
- If you answered yes to any of the above, evaluate with a view to exit the party.

Helpful tips

Know the address of the place you are attending the party off head- in case you need to quickly exit.

Keep a keen watch on your drinks, do not leave them open to go to the bathroom or dancing floor.

Have a list of quick dials in case you need to safely call someone without alarming people around you.

Conclusion:

No matter what your category is, in a relationship and not sure if it is working well or not, not in a relationship, or committed in a very promising relationship, there are things we can do to improve or maintain healthy relationships. There are other things we can do to help those in our families, in our schools and colleges, our communities, religious organizations develop and maintain healthy relationships. Everybody deserves a healthy relationship and the great thing is that it is achievable, because there are skills one can learn to succeed.

It is my hope that this guide helps you look back into your relationship and find ways to strengthen it. Whatever you do, keep safe, ensure safety of friends whenever you can and if in doubt, call for help.

Notes

1   Donna Dale Carnegie, *How to Win Friends & Influence People for Teen Girls,* (Simon & Schuster, 2005) New York, NY

2   Gary Chapman, *The Five Love Languages of Teenagers,* (Moody Publishers, 2000), Chicago, Illinois

3   Gary Chapman, *Love is a verb*, (Bethany House Publishers, 2009), Minneapolis, Minnesota

4   http://www.endabuse.com/retrieved February 9,2012

5   http://www.loveisrespect.org/dating-basics/healthy-relationships/ retrieved February 9, 2012

6   http://www.loveisnotabuse.com/retrieved February 8,2012

7   Love Notes, *Making Relationships work for young adults and young parents*, (Dibble Institute, 2009) Berkeley, CA.

Answers: Choosing greens versus reds

- The first thing you do is to remove the blindfold, then you can pick from the green bowl

- You can decide to choose from bowl one instead of bowl two, that way you have high chances of choosing a green.

- If you must choose from bowl two, you can decide to remove some reds or add some greens.

- In life you must make decisions, if you are choosing a friend, you must weigh the company you keep. If it is more in the red, you must deliberately start adding more greens in your life and removing some reds. This means you have to quit friendships or company that deters your success and keep or build

About the Author

 **Rose W. Muraguri** lives in Raleigh, NC with her husband, Dr. Robert Muraguri and their three daughters Christine, Quincy and Pressy. Rose has an MA in Marriage & Family, B Ed in Education and has worked extensively in the area of relationship strengthening, with both the youth and married couples. Before dedicating her career to enhancing relationships, Rose worked as a high school teacher for 14 years where she also offered voluntary guidance and counseling to high school youth. She has traveled extensively here in the USA, Europe and Africa, offering seminars and workshops to youth and adults. As Programs Director of TISNA; an NGO in North Carolina, Rose started a TV program in January 2012, which focuses on strengthening relations and peaceful coexistence between immigrants and the host American community. Currently, she directs and hosts *The Trumpet* TV program. Rose is also active in church ministries with special interest in youth and women affairs.

2656093R00040

Printed in Germany
by Amazon Distribution
GmbH, Leipzig